Race Track Attack Guide

Buttonwillow Raceway Park

(Configuration No. 13 Clockwise)

The Enthusiast's Approach to the High Performance Driving Experience on America's Road Racing Courses

Edwin Reeser, III

Sericin Publishing Company

Copyright 2010, Sericin Publishing Company

All rights reserved. World rights reserved. No part of this book may be reproduced in any form or by any means, electronic or mechanical, including photocopying, recording or by any information storage and retrieval system, without the prior written permission of Sericin Publishing Company, except in the case of brief passages embodied in critical reviews or articles.

ISBN Number: 978-0-9841724-2-9

Library of Congress Control Number: 2010906168

DISCLAIMER: The contents of this book are true to the best knowledge of the author. All recommendations are made without guarantee on the part of the author or the publisher. The author and the publisher disclaim any liability incurred in connection with the use of any data or recommendations in this book. In particular, no portion of this book should be taken to suggest or condone the violation of any traffic laws or the practice of any unsafe driving.

Printed in the United States of America

All maps used to illustrate the Buttonwillow driving lines are from Matthew Reeser and Kathryn Marcellino.

All photos are from Edwin Reeser.

A publication of Sericin Publishing Company, Sericin Management, LLC.

Matthew Reeser, Editor in Chief

Contents

Foreword 5
Introduction 7
The Track 11
Perspective 13
Track Entry 23
The Sunrise Turn 29
The Offramp Turn 33
The Cotton Corners 39
Grapevine Turn 45
The Club Corner 49
The Bus Stop Turn 53
Truck Stop and the Riverside Sweeper 57
Approach to Phil Hill 63
Phil Hill 67
Approach to Sweeper 71
Sweeper 73
The Esses 77
Prepare for the Unexpected 85
The Sunset Turn 93
Track Exit 95
Distinguishing Characteristics 99
Conclusion 101
Closing Note on Driving Lines 103
Track Checklist 105
Tech Inspection Form 109
Dedication 110
Acknowledgement 111
About the Author 112
Other Titles by Sericin Publishing 113

Foreword

Having worked with Ed Reeser at Nissan Sport magazine, I know how keen he is for detail. While most of us stumble through motorsports and life (those two inseparable endeavors) relying on our meager talents, Ed is constantly on the lookout for the smallest details. When he turns his attention to each racetrack, his ability to analyze the topography of the circuit, together with his explanation as to *why* each detail is important can be more valuable than gold.

Perhaps just as important is the display of a thinking man's approach to motorsports. In my twenty-odd years of being an active racer, I've witnessed just how critical this aspect of driving has become. Beyond purely technological aides such as state-of-the-art data acquisition, each participant can get the most out of their track day experience by flexing that most important muscle—the one located between their ears—before, during and after the event. And as you read about balancing risk vs. reward through each corner of the track, you'll begin to appreciate Ed's successful approach to high-performance driving.

Beyond that, and even if you use this book to gain greater insight into specific corners or areas of the track you are having difficulty with, Ed offers side notes and suggestions that are well-worth paying attention to. Most of us have learned these lessons through years of bent fenders, busted wheels or worse. I'd suggest reading and re-reading his descriptions slowly to give yourself time to assimilate this information. Once you hit the track, things will happen quickly and you will be faced with making split second decisions that could impact (pun intended) your ability to continue a pleasant day.

Finally, Ed makes the point that no tangible rewards (trophies, points or money) are part of a typical track day or HPDE. But I disagree. The reward that each successful participant takes home at the end of the day is the beautiful, shining car of your dreams. Hopefully, the same one you drove to the track in! And beyond this, it's my belief that each successful lap—driven to the limit of our abilities—transforms us as individuals. Making us more aware of the capabilities of our vehicles and what we can and cannot do, is a priceless experience. Have a great day at the track!

David Muramoto
Editor-in-chief
Nissan Sport Magazine

Buttonwillow Raceway Park

Introduction

Located about a two hour drive north of Los Angeles on Interstate 5, then a left turn and one half mile west on the Lerdo Highway, Buttonwillow Raceway Park is a versatile layout that can be driven either direction in multiple configurations. This article will describe a lap around the three mile, 23 turn configuration #13, run clockwise, which is popular for many competitions and High Performance Driving Experience ("HPDE") events.

Built, owned and operated by the California Sports Car Club (CSCC), Southern California Region of the Sports Car Club of America, Buttonwillow opened for operations in 1996. The facility is at a relatively low 250 foot elevation above sea level, and is flat, excepting two small man made "hills" at opposite ends of the circuit and a small but abrupt "rise" following the Grapevine corner.

This Track Attack analysis will present the driver with a tool to help prepare for a high performance driving lap at Buttonwillow Raceway Park, including track entry and track exit procedure.

One should always do a track map study of a circuit before driving the course, view in car videos, look at still photographs of corners and features, and even play a video game simulation, as well as talk to drivers and instructors well experienced with the track. However, none of these will adequately convey the sensory sensations from the rush of air and sound from the engine and tires as you hurtle down the front straight, the deceleration pressure on the chest through application of braking before making a hard right corner turn in to the bowl banking of "Offramp", the rapid lateral transfers through the Cotton Corners culminating in an angled hill crest, the tightrope balance of staying on track through the Bus Stop corner, the high speed carousel of the Riverside turn, the weightless crest over Phil Hill, the tight late apex after the Sweeper, threading the Esses, and the tires squealing through oversteer in the Sunset Turn as you enter the front straight.

This configuration has twenty three corners in approximately three miles. While top speeds will not be as high as some circuits because of the undulations and corners, powerful cars will reach speeds in excess of 135 mph on this configuration. But first and foremost this is a teaching track, a course from which you will learn a great deal if you pay attention. A course that demands and rewards superior driving techniques in car control (steering, braking, weight transfer), and gear changing footwork. If you have weaknesses in your high performance driving technique, Buttonwillow will unmask them. Under proper supervision and sponsorship, this course is accessible to most drivers at this writing.

While a chance to drive any car on a race track is usually great fun, that might not be the case at any track absent a well organized event, and the great majority of event sponsors at Buttonwillow fortunately attend to this carefully. Before selecting your event sponsor to run with at Buttonwillow, be sure you confirm that they follow a disciplined safety orientation for all drivers.

This is not a track configuration that favors high horsepower cars. That does not mean you won't have a great time with a high powered car on this track. Only that driver skill combined with a well handling vehicle is more important than brute force at Buttonwillow's Race #13 in the clockwise direction. This is a track where you can frequently see a Spec Miata with a good driver thrash a Corvette with a mediocre driver. Vipers, Corvettes and other powerful cars will have a great time at Buttonwillow, as there are sections that do provide the opportunity to unleash the beast under that long hood... but their drivers will have an even better time the more skillful they are.

(**Beginner's note:** Most organizations managing a HPDE on Buttonwillow carefully separate run groups during event registration not only by driver skill and experience, but also by types and capabilities of cars, so that closer comparability of lap times will ensure a day of running that is more safe and fun for all participants. Be sure when you organize your track day, that you confirm there will be a novice group, with instructors, and no mixing of cars that will result in widely disparate speeds for your group.)

This course can be a bit humiliating for the novice that has not yet developed the skills to effectively heel/toe downshift and rev match, rotate or yaw the car into a turn, trail brake, left foot brake, etc. That is in no small part because inherent in the design of this course is the requirement that you learn these skills to drive it well.

Buttonwillow is not a course you drive once. It is a course you drive again and again, and the better you get, the more rewarding and fun it becomes.

The Track

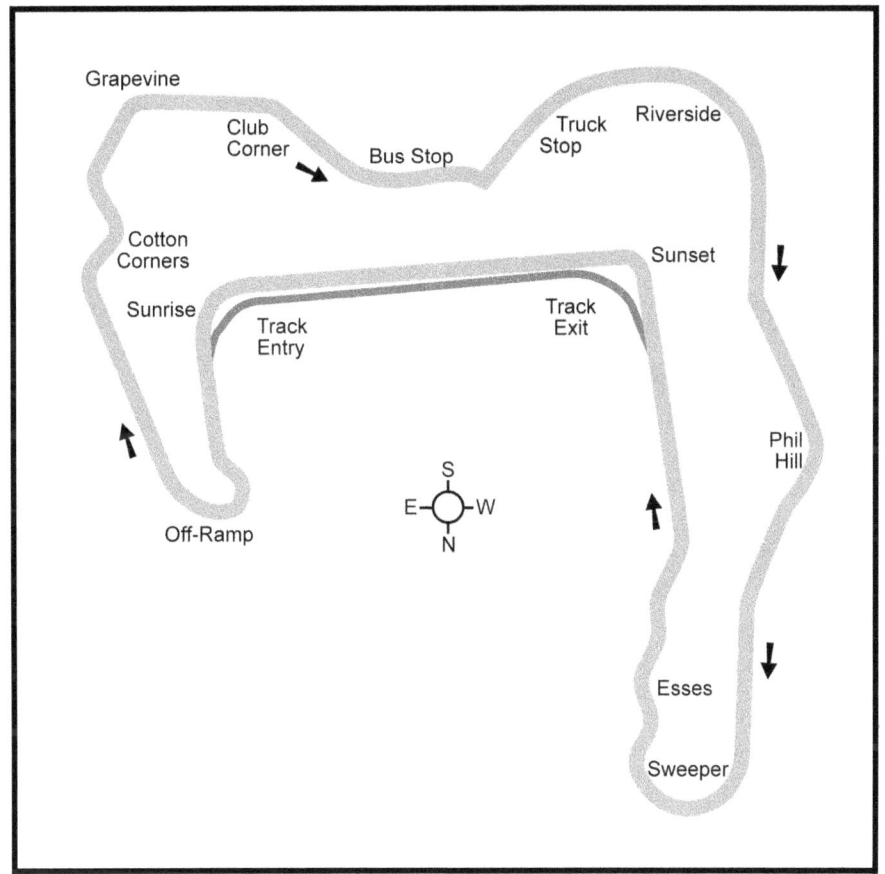

Note the right to left inertia and "light" rear of lead car leaving apex on top of Phil Hill.

Perspective

Reality Check: Before we get into how to enjoy High Performance Driving Education ("HPDE") and the track notes for Buttonwillow, a few words about what this experience is about and its risks.

Many sports involve highly developed skills where you throw, catch, strike, or kick a ball. If you make a mistake the result typically involves a lost point, a change in possession, a replay, or perhaps a lost ball and a "do over" with a scoring penalty, and the game continues. *In high performance driving, you are the ball, and there are no second chances.* Accordingly, driving the "ball" over the fence or into the lake is not an option.

Some sports have a significant potential of serious injury or death if things go wrong. You may do everything right yourself, and still get caught by the mistakes of others or unpredictable events. Mountain and free climbing, scuba diving, sky diving, spelunking, bungee jumping, hang gliding, bull fighting and driving a car, motorcycle or bicycle fast all can have seriously negative consequences, irrespective of fault. If introducing even a moment of inattention to a relatively safer activity, such as crossing a street on foot, can be fatal, (stepping into the path of a bus while reading the morning paper, for example) then it is clear that a moment of inattention in one of the aforementioned activities is potentially more so.

All sports require a detailed level of knowledge and practice to perform well. Striking a golf ball is not an inherently natural series of coordinated actions. Neither is throwing, catching or hitting a baseball, climbing the face of a rock wall, or making a controlled sky diving free fall. HPDE driving is most definitely an undertaking that benefits from serious study of the geometry of tracks, the components and working of your car, the art of driving, safety considerations at all levels, and physical and mental preparation of the driver. You will drive better and be safer if you devote the time and energy to do it right by studying, and practice.

Driving a car is an inherently dangerous activity. Driving a car fast, even under the best of conditions and preparation in a well-controlled track situation, is even more so. A 3000 pound car moving at 60 mph has the potential energy to move a 5,808 TON block of concrete one foot. That car moving at 120 mph has the energy to move a

23,232 TON block of concrete one foot. A speed of 120 mph is not really "fast" in the auto racing world. There are numerous circuits where a street car can reach speeds of as much as 150 mph, or more. As kinetic energy increases as the square of speed, twice as fast means four times the energy. If there is a problem on the street or the track, all that energy has to go someplace before your car comes to a stop. If it is dissipated through braking to a smooth stop it is highly desirable, as contrasted with a series of violent roll over strikes upon the ground or against a concrete wall. This is especially true if the concrete wall does not move and the energy is absorbed by the compression of the car with *you* inside of it.

As you spend more time on the track, the odds of having an unpleasant experience will tend to catch up with you. You will exit the track surface, lose control of your car or have someone lose control of their car in front of you. All people make errors in judgment. All things mechanical and electrical can and eventually will break or fail. Random events can and do suddenly occur. They have happened to me, and all of the other drivers that I know, so there is no reasonable expectation that you will escape this fundamental reality any more than you can defy the laws of gravity.

But you can prepare to make the best of it when bad things happen. Part of the focus of this book is to bring to light how you approach driving and maintaining your car, and whether you may need to consider changing your approach to make yourself a safer driver on the street and track. You may find that track experience can benefit you on the street, keep you out of trouble. Not because you can drive faster than others, but because you are more aware, have developed additional car control skills, and can get the most out of your car and yourself in an emergency.

If you cannot accept the responsibility or consequences of driving on a race track, don't do it. Driving a car under the laws applicable in all licensing jurisdictions that I am aware of is not a right, it is a privilege, and you are responsible to do everything you reasonably can to prevent damage to your car, the cars of others and/or injury to yourself or others. That is just for street use of a car. On a track, the safety and preparation expectations and requirements of most sponsoring organizations is even higher, and the assumptions of the risk that you take for your actions, and those of others, is higher as well. Nobody is forcing you to drive on the track, and certainly you should not allow anybody to persuade you to do it. Thoroughly investigate and study first, and then make up your own mind.

Once you have made the decision that you are going to drive a car on a race track, then it is your responsibility to do it as safely and intelligently as you can, for your own sake and that of those around you. Such care includes your careful preparation of the car, its transport to and from the track, and staging in the garage and pits. It includes your personal skill development and preparation through driving schools and practice in car control on and off the track. It also includes how you enter the track, how you leave the track at the end of your session, how you evaluate the risk areas of the track and develop your plans to deal with those risks.

Be mentally, emotionally and physically prepared for the stresses. The level of concentration required is more intense and sustained than any driving experience you have had on the street, and possibly more than any other experience you have ever had anywhere. The faster you go, the more data you have to deal with, and the less time and distance to deal with it, and however good you think you are, or actually are, sooner or later you will find you are not good enough at some point, in some corner, on some day. That is not good or bad. It is just the way it is.

While you cannot eliminate all of the risks associated with high performance driving, you can do a lot to reduce and to manage risks by proper preparation of yourself and your car, attention to safety at all levels of equipment and driving techniques, and by running with reputable organizations and sponsors of track day events. Please do all of that and more.

The satisfaction that comes from driving a very fast lap derives from an assembly of many little things. It takes time, practice and study to get it right, and patience is a virtue. Fast driving does not come from deciding that you want to drive "fast" and stepping harder on the gas and brake pedals of a car with a big engine. Rather it comes from developing the car control and driving skills to accelerate, turn, brake, shift and balance weight on the car ***smoothly and precisely*** under a wide array of differing conditions and circumstances. As you improve those skills... speeds increase, lap times decrease, and more importantly your errors should decrease. Slow is *smooth*, and smooth becomes *fast*.

What defines "fast" is what is fast for you. Compared to a horse, you will be going very fast, and for a turtle... even more so. Yet for a beam of light or radio wave you will be virtually stationary! As to other drivers... don't get trapped into that element of competition. It is of no emotional importance that somebody else in a different car is a few seconds slower or faster than you.

If you want to be competitive against others in your driving, and there are many people who do, there are organizations that arrange competitions for "time attack" or racing against the clock versus other drivers, as well as the traditional and popular "wheel to wheel" racing. Those are not HPDE and should not be confused with HPDE. If you want to do that type of competitive driving, get yourself into a proper racing organization and follow their program.

In HPDE, there is no blood, honor or money on the table. No fashion beauties with bouquets of flowers, no gigantic bottles of champagne to spray adoring fans, no poster sized checks for amazing sums of money, await you for being the fastest driver on the track.

The goal is to learn to drive as skillfully as you can as safely as you can at speeds within the capabilities of yourself, the car, and the track under the specific conditions of the day, and then go home at day's end with car and body unscathed.

Do not be dismissive of the repeated emphasis in this analysis on technical car control issues associated with this circuit, as the purpose is to help you know where to focus to manage speed and car control, especially in sections like Bus Stop, Riverside, Lost Hill and Sweeper. Going fast, and going fast *safely*, are not the same thing. Any person, and many trained animals, can get behind the wheel of a powerful car, hold the wheel straight and put the accelerator to the floor. You must not mistake the capabilities engineered into the car to be an extension of your capabilities as a driver, especially with respect to car control at speed.

Having a fast car and being a fast driver are two unrelated statements of fact.

Know your limitations.

Driving this course is terrific fun, but you must recognize and respect the limitations of the track, the car, and yourself with clarity. While most beginners approach track days with the reserve and caution appropriate to reduce risk of mishap, there is so much technically going on in short periods of time and distance at Buttonwillow that a novice can easily run out of track surface, control options and ideas all at the same time. Fortunately, the course has a lot of run off room in most sections, and speeds do not tend to be quite as extreme as some other circuits. Do not be frustrated by the challenges of car control you discover driving this track either. As a novice with only two days of driving experience on two other tracks, and filled with enthusiasm and excitement about this new found joy of HPDE, my first experience driving Buttonwillow was one of strong disappointment in the discovery of just how wanting in driver skills I was. That is one of the reasons it is designed the way it is, and the practice and skill development you can have at Buttonwillow make it one of the best courses you can drive, at any level of skill. Notwithstanding the relatively slower speeds overall, there remain risks on this track for the intermediate and advanced drivers who are pushing the envelope of performance limits for their cars, and their own driving skills, at higher speeds in Riverside, Phil Hill and Bus Stop where the consequences of loss of control are more severe, with a roll over possibility. Cars dropping two wheels to the right edge on exit from the Esses have launched cross track left into the wall with some frequency, as have those going off track to the right exiting the Sunset Turn gone into the wall separating the front straight from the paddock and hot pit lane. Control recovery at high speed is always more difficult, and the consequences of lost control to driver and machine more severe, so respect this attribute of speed when driving Buttonwillow, where corners that are technically simple at slower speeds like Riverside, Bus Stop, Phil Hill and Sweeper develop subtle nuances at higher speeds that can surprise the driver.

Car on left has taken "point by" passing opportunity in Club Corner transition, as passed car has held out from the driving line on right to give more passing room. We shall hold position and give room to car on right to safely reacquire the driving line, follow them through the Bus Stop Turn, then pass the car exiting the Truck Stop Turn while entering the Riverside sweeper, once more with a point by signal from the lead car.

Track Entry

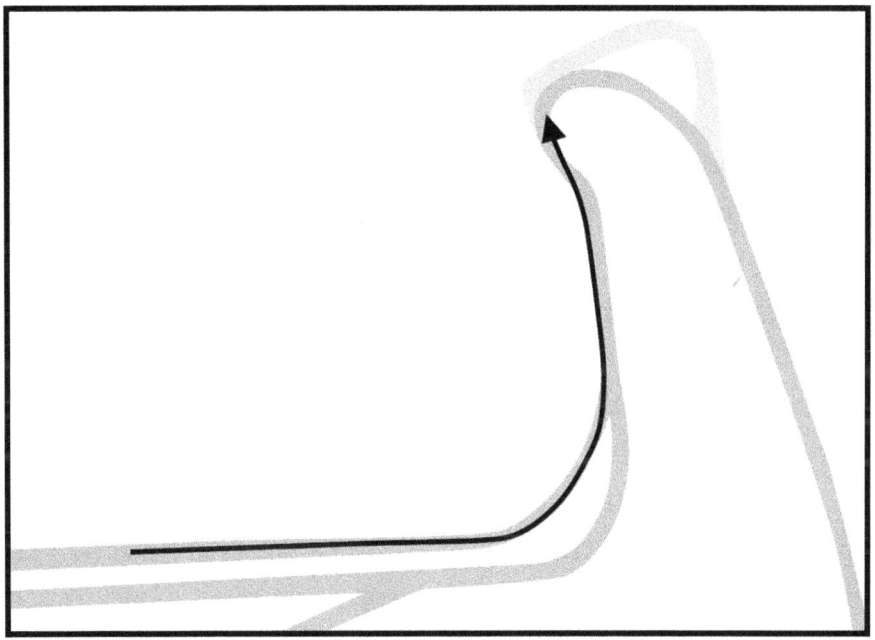

Safety for both the entering car and the cars on track is a priority for every road course and participant. Every track has a unique set of issues associated with its track entry and its track exit. You need to study and understand both track entry and exit procedure and technique *before* you show up.

Given the intersection of driving lines between entering cars and on track cars shortly after track entry at Buttonwillow, special attention must be paid to this aspect of driving the course, both from the perspective of the entering car, and the on track car encountering a merge from the entry lane as the driving lines of both cars blend together.

Track Entry begins from the extreme left, with the starter stationed below the control room on the second floor of the club building at the start/finish line, and separated from the "hot pit" lane by a concrete k rail wall on the right. Drivers will grid their cars in either single or double file format at the starting grid at the direction of the starter. Drivers are typically called to the grid for their driving session ten minutes before the scheduled start, and should all be present by not later than three minutes before the scheduled start. The starter or assistant starter should check wrist bands to confirm that all drivers on the grid are in the proper session group and qualified to participate in that session, and to pass along any last minute information ("there is a dropped bit of coolant from a car at the right edge of the track surface on exit from Bus Stop. It will be mopped and sanded when the current session on the track ends, and before you start, but the debris flag will be taken down so be aware that it is still there"). While you are on the start grid, cars may come and go from the hot pit lane from the current session on track.

The track entry lane runs parallel to the front straight, and then cuts inside the first corner (the Sunrise Turn), putting the car on the left edge of the track in front of the corner entry to the left to right Offramp Turn. As driver of the entering car, use your peripheral vision as you gather speed on entry, and your mirrors, as you curve left, to pick up any cars approaching from the front straight or entering the Sunrise Turn.

As you enter on the left edge of the track surface, cars on track approaching from behind will be on the right side exiting the Sunrise Turn. However, they will be transitioning from right to left directly behind you, accelerating on corner exit and then braking across an entry corner apex on the left edge for the subsequent entry to the sharp left to right Offramp Turn, so be aware of your surroundings.

The danger zone for potential collision on entry to the track is not at the point of entry, but rather the space immediately preceding the right to left entry to the Offramp Turn. The closure rate between entering cars and cars on track is not extreme as the corner entry speed is relatively slow (a good design feature!). The danger at track entry is in the point of decision by the overtaking car to pass to the right of the entering car and reach the braking zone first, or to slow down and slip behind the entering car.

Unlike many race courses, this turn entry area leads to one of the slowest turns on the track, so the entering car will be able to achieve a speed in excess of what may be carried into and through the corner before it gets to the corner. A touch of complication, however, is added by the fact that the optimal entry angle to the corner is from the right side of the track surface, while the entering car should hug the left edge, and thus corner entry speed for the on track car will be slightly higher than for the entering car, and the radius arc for the left to right turn input for the on track car will be slightly longer and faster following corner entry.

(**Beginner's note:** It is tempting for the entering car to wander wide right to get onto the optimal driving line and thus improve the angle of entry to the Offramp. However, you must resist that temptation and *hold to the entry line* because you may have failed to pick up the approach from behind of an on track car, and by moving to the optimal on track driving line from the entry lane you will be creeping left to right and directly into the passing line of a faster moving car.)

With respect to the actual point of entry on the track, Buttonwillow has as safe an entry clockwise as any road course designed. Speeds are moderate, and both entering and on track cars have time and space to see each other, and if necessary to make adjustments. And they are initially oriented at opposite sides of the track surface. However, every track has at least one point where the driving line of the entering cars and the driving line of the on track cars "blend" together, and this is a primary risk point, though not necessarily the only one. Both the entering cars and cars on track must pay careful attention to the dynamic of entering cars. It is, as always, the responsibility of the overtaking car to make a safe pass, and for the entering car to follow a predictable entry driving line and speed.

Front straight. It is the responsibility of the overtaking car to complete a safe pass.

Entry from right edge to late apex.

Full throttle at apex. Note how quickly track out takes you to right edge.

The Sunrise Turn

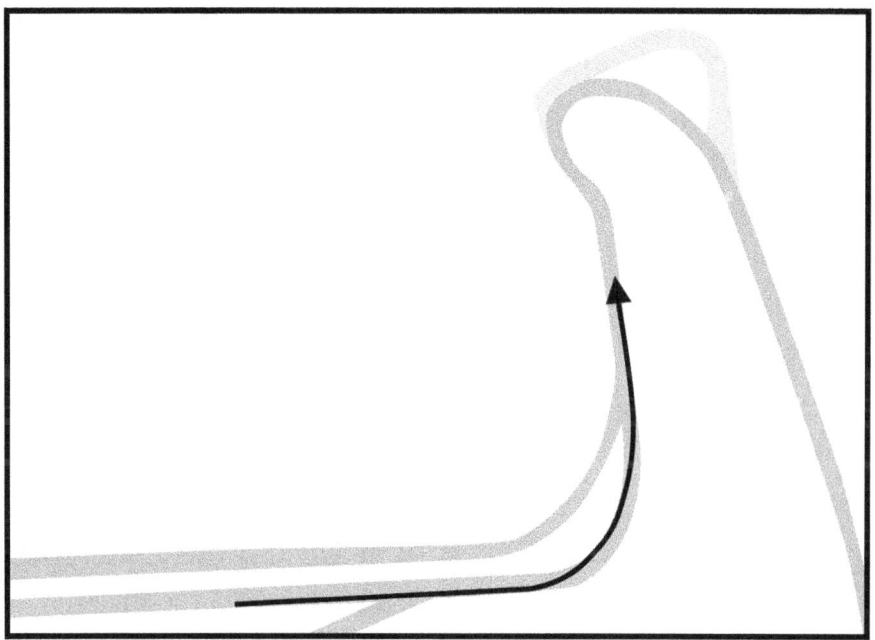

As you begin your run down the front straight at Buttonwillow, you will be on the right edge of the track heading eastward. The straight has a couple of small "undulations" in the surface that can unsettle the car just a touch at high speed, so a steady, but not tight, grip on the steering wheel is advisable. Up shift from either third or fourth gear depending on your selection going into the final corner, named "Sunset", grab fourth or fifth gear before you cross the start/finish line, scan the entry lane on the left for any cars that you may encounter on your approach to Offramp, check your gauges, check your mirror for anyone that is behind you and potentially will be gaining on you in the straight or next busy segments, then begin your straight braking on the right edge and heel/toe downshift to fourth or even third gear. You can carry higher speed through Sunrise in the clockwise direction than often expected, and it is followed by a short straight, so be smooth with the pedal and don't upset the car balance with a late "over brake".

(Beginner's note: The Sunrise Turn is about 100 degrees, reasonably high speed, and with very little camber, so take a late turn in for corner entry and a late apex. As you accelerate out expect the right edge to come up just a bit quickly on your track out during corner exit compared to what you would typically expect with a 90 degree corner. You will frequently get some tire squeal here as you work your grip to the limits of adhesion. Keep your head up and swiveled left through the apex point to the track out target, and this will help you unwind your steering lock in a smooth, flowing release through the corner without running off the right edge. If you keep your vision down looking off the hood of the car into the apex point, you can be surprised during track out as there is a natural tendency to unwind steering a bit earlier for a ninety degree turn, and if you do that you will possibly run off the right edge, or make sudden adjustments that will either slow you down, or potentially cause you control problems).

Stay on right edge and resist temptation to creep left off the driving line

Straight brake with left wheels across stripes in driving line that bisects pavement to set up corner entry.

Sharp left to right entry. Begin acceleration into apex and corner camber.

The Offramp Turn

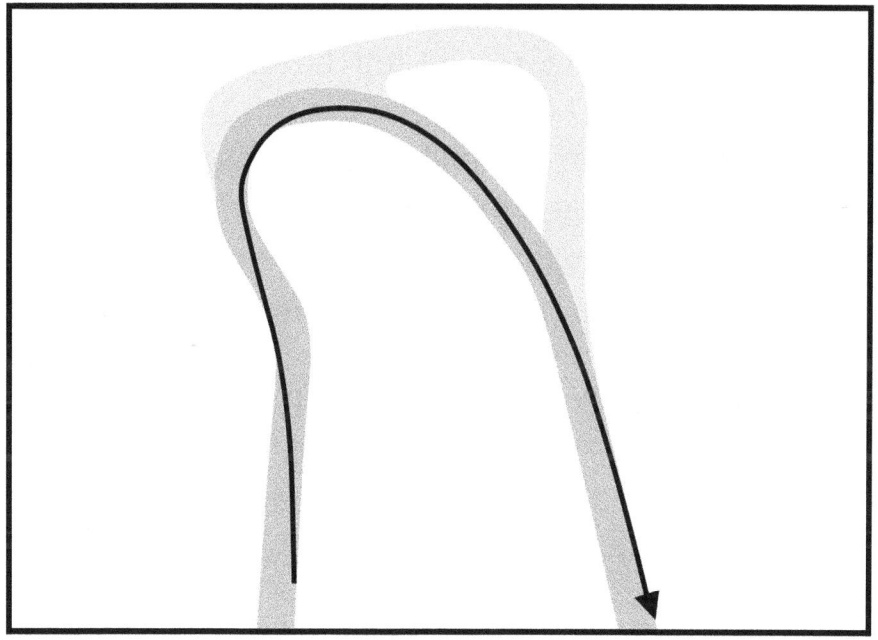

You now approach a compound left/right corner called "Offramp". Though not nearly as difficult a corner when run in the clockwise direction, there is not a corner out there that you cannot manage to exit unceremoniously, and it merits close attention to run smoothly as it leads to a medium length straight.

Stay to the right edge after exiting Sunrise. Scan quickly to the left edge for the entry lane to pick up any cars entering the track and determine whether you will need to adjust your speed or driving line to avoid intersection during the corner entry to Offramp. Resist the temptation to pinch in or "crab" to the left early as you approach the corner entry on the left edge. Instead, hold to the right edge as long as possible under full throttle, take a late turn in to the left hand "kink" of the corner entry, and then apply a short, hard thresh hold braking run in a straight line across and through the corner entry apex point on the left, and simultaneously execute your heel/toe downshifts.

At present the braking zone has quite a number of patches and surface differences, so the combination of differing surfaces under braking, shifting and turning, especially for the advanced drivers in fast cars working the limits of their wider tires and stiffer suspension spring rates, can make the car dance a little Irish jig here as the tires and suspension fight for adhesion.

This approach should set yourself up for carrying a bit more speed deeply to the corner by allowing you, when you do brake, to use all of the grip for braking rather than some for turn in and some for braking at the same time on a dodgy surface. In addition, the surface dips slightly down and drops a couple of feet in elevation after this entry apex as you prepare to make your left to right steering input.

Offramp is a rapidly expanding short radius corner and has a significant positive "bowl" camber working to your favor early in the corner. You can get on the throttle earlier and harder than the overhead look at the track map would suggest. This approach will orient the car for a slightly earlier turn in for this right hand corner that the bowl will permit you to take and still hold the driving line. You may with aggressive early throttle attack on Offramp get some rear rotation as the corner radius opens out, the positive camber goes away, and you pass over a small crest, reducing the grip of the rear tires and promoting a throttle on over steer, so be ready to quick counter steer while you stay in the throttle through this section. Unwind your steering a bit more rapidly as the positive camber goes away to reduce the grip demand for turning on the tires, and track out to the left edge of the pavement.

(**Beginner's note:** this is a hairpin corner so swivel your head like a barn owl 90 degrees to the right and focus on your exit mark before you begin your turn in. It is very easy in a tight corner like Offramp to be driving the corner while looking off the nose of your car, or even looking nervously to the left at the orange cones demarking the edge of the track, which will materially slow you down from your potential and put you into a "reactive" driving mode of what you see a few feet in front of you rather than a "command" mode based on anticipation of what you can see is coming far ahead.

The path the car follows will tend to follow the path of your eyes. If you are darting your vision up and down and side to center and back, you will compromise your corner exit speed, probably make your driving line wobble or vary instead of being smooth in its arc, upset the balance of the car through multiple slight weight transfers and generally make hash of driving the entire corner.

Keep your chin and eyes up, swivel your head and fix your vision towards the track out and let the nose of the car follow around to your target as you concentrate on throttle pressure and steering feel, and you should be amazed at the improvement in smoothness and speed you acquire in this corner, and how much easier it becomes to drive. This is a great slow speed lesson in how you *command* the car through anticipation of what the car needs, as contrasted with having the car tell you and *reacting* to it, which is much too late to be able to drive through it smoothly or quickly. It takes time for driving inputs to be physically effected by you the driver, and more time for the car to react to them. Any time on a race track is distance traveled, and the faster you are going, the greater that distance. At higher velocities, the turn inputs are well before you get to the point where you want the car responding to those inputs.)

Hold steering into turn and increase acceleration.

Note flat camber and increasing radius; flow to exit apex on right.

Unwind steering and smoothly transition towards left edge.

Late entry to align on right edge following first corner.

The Cotton Corners

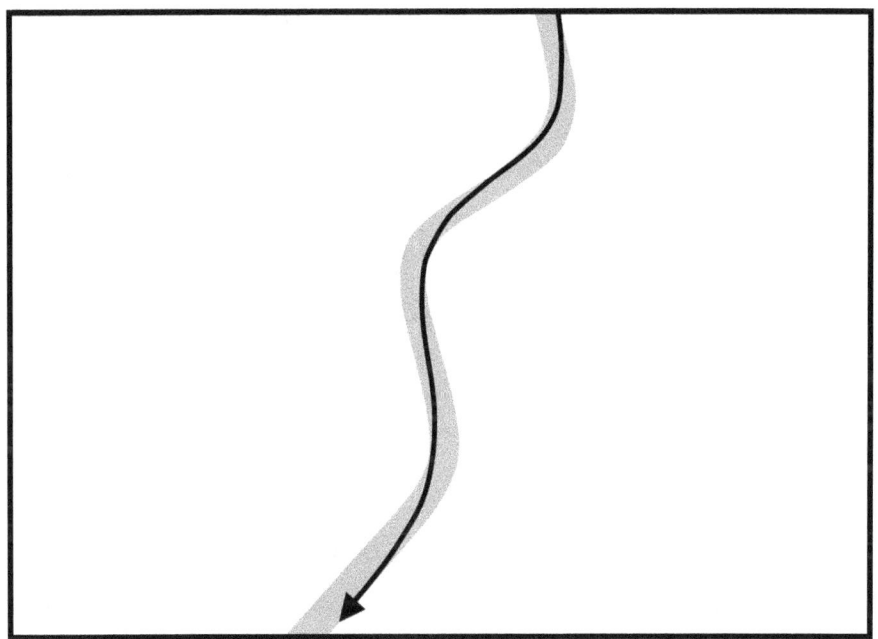

As you track out to the left edge corner exit from Offramp, and continue hard acceleration down the left side of the track for entry to the "Cotton Corners" you will up shift once and in some cars briefly twice. (You may have to choose to stay in gear at redline and extend for a second or two rather than up shift). Where an advanced driver may have the wheels of their car aligned precisely along the edge of the track surface or a couple of inches from it, a beginner should leave a safe margin of two or even three feet all around the track. Give yourself some more room to work with. As your abilities improve, you can gradually reduce the margins, and be adjusting your reference points in terms of inches). No matter what your experience level, always stay safely within your limits as a driver, the limits of the car you are driving, and the condition of the track.

The Cotton Corners is a compound corner trio, a right-left-right combination, incorporating an abrupt climb of about twenty feet between the second and third corners with the apex of the third corner just at or slightly over the crest of the hill. Maximizing corner exit speed at the third corner is your objective in this segment. Overcooking your entry to the first corner will ruin the entire segment, and the segment to follow.

Your approach to Cotton Corners is to straight brake, heel/toe down shift, and with just a touch of trail brake rotate the rear of the car into the first of the three corners, so that you can stay close to the right side of the track edge as you cut across a very late apex with both right side wheels in the first corner. Stay on throttle along the right edge towards the second corner of this trio, then just a short stab at the brake and heel/toe downshift and transfer some weight forward, and turn left through the second corner. You can get some trail brake rotation here as well, as this is perhaps the slowest turn on the track. This will help to yaw the nose around and stay on the left edge of the track as you exit the second corner.

Now you have a choice, to either push through in your present gear selection, or quick up shift and then make your turn in to the last corner, depending on your gearing selection going into Cotton Corners. Make the apex to this third corner LATE, under full throttle, and straighten the steering just as you crest, because as you crest the hill the momentum will make the rear light and any lateral momentum or applying steering will throw the rear end of the car to the left, on an off camber descent, and that of course can spin you out, potentially leaving you broadside to the next car coming blind over the hill.

If you early apex the corner you cannot carry speed without running off the track, and you have almost no choice but to lift throttle or even brake slightly going up the little hill... causing some front to back "porpoising" and broadcasting an immensely frustrating confession of a technically bad driving line and corner entry technique at low speed. All this of course mandates that you ALWAYS note the flag station at the right of the hill crest as you come through Cotton Corners, looking for the yellow flag to warn of that possible condition of a car spun out in front of you. If you are close on the tail of another car, be mindful of his rear wheel grip and the signs that he may lose control so you don't run up his tailpipe if he lifts throttle or applies brake going up grade into the hill, or into his door if he starts to spin on the far side. You don't need to be crowding anybody anywhere on a track during HPDE, but especially not here.

(Beginner's note: Squeeze your throttle on smoothly as you come towards the top of the hill crest to settle the back and gain more grip, then steer straight over the crest as you flow to the left edge of the track surface, which even though you are not moving through at high speed comes to you quickly. Ease the steering to the right as the back of the car settles. As soon as the car grips and aligns with the left edge, unwind your steering, accelerate hard and if you did not up shift before the crest of the hill, do it now as you approach the Grapevine.)

Both right wheels across edge of stripes and hold to right edge.

Late entry to set up third corner. Note center left position of lead car at turn in.

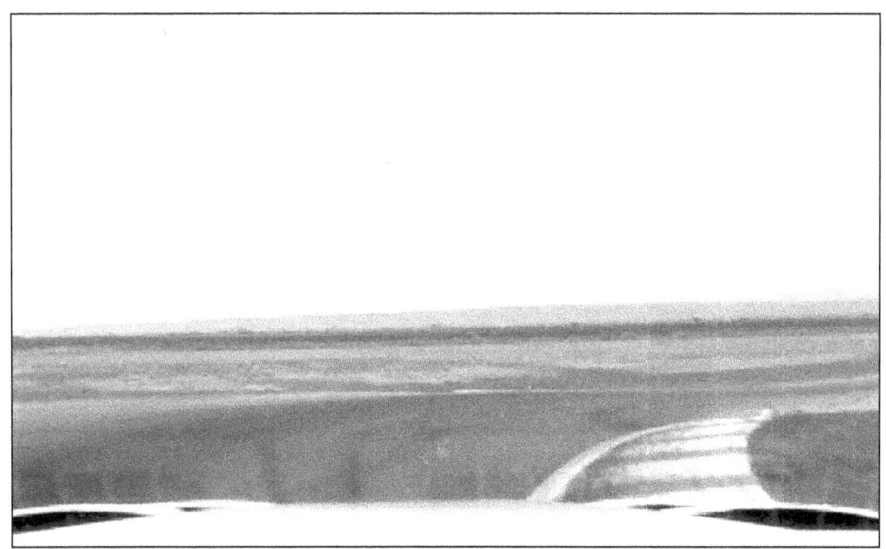

Straighten steering at top and through apex, track out left on exit.

Accelerate and prepare for Grapevine corner turn in.

Grapevine Turn

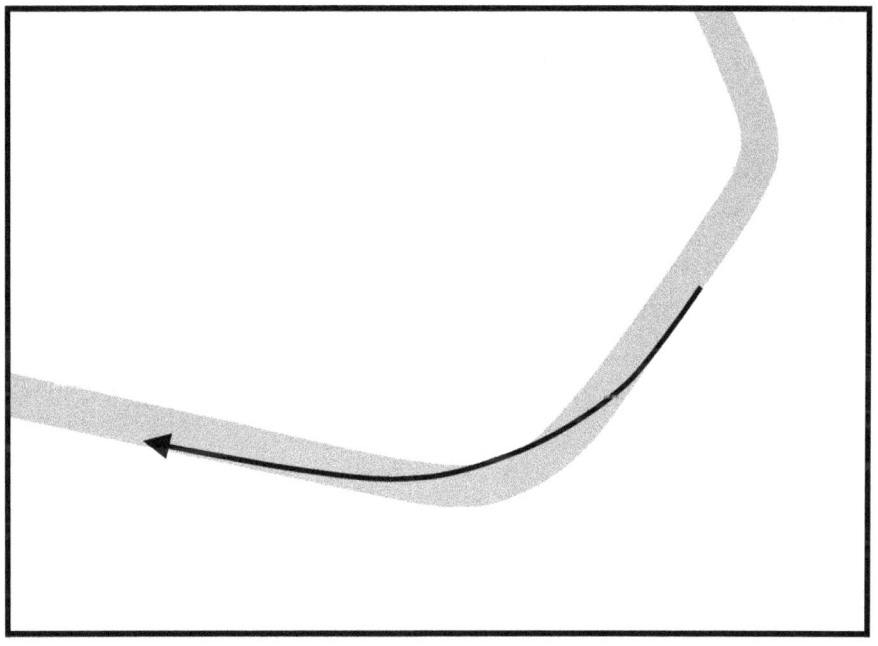

Grapevine is about an 80 degree left to right corner on a flat to slightly off camber surface. You will be accelerating down the short segment after Cotton Corners and if you have negotiated that segment well, you will see that you can carry the extra speed all the way through Grapevine, the Club Corner and into Bus Stop... so it is almost the same as if the track all the way down to Bus Stop is a straight for many cars.

Thus an error in Cotton Corners punishes the driver for the next two turns with the lost exit speed.

Grapevine is not a corner that typically requires braking before entry. At most for a very high horsepower car it might require just a breathe off throttle or a touch of left foot brake to move some weight forward followed by a squeeze back on as the car takes a "set" on turn in from left to right. Instead, the Grapevine turn is much about the limits of adhesion of your tires and how much throttle you can apply without losing rear traction in a power induced or "throttle on" over steer.

What becomes additionally challenging is the abrupt change in elevation, not visible on the track map, as you exit the Grapevine ...about a four foot rise just when you are preparing to up shift. Depending on your car and gearing you will have to choose to complete that shift just before or just after the "hump". There is a strong temptation to lift throttle and you need to resist that and stay Wide Open Throttle ("WOT") into and through that abrupt incline.

(**Beginner's note:** This is an excellent corner to experience throttle on over steer in a relatively safer location on the track. No walls, ample run off space, wide open visibility in front and behind, and moderate speed on a less than 90 degree turn. There is, relatively speaking, room to recover, and with your instructor you can ask him/her to show you how the car behaves and how to recover if it starts to slip in this section. That does not mean go out and hammer it the first time you drive the course! It is not unlike Turn 4 at Laguna Seca, but at about 30-50 mph higher velocity difference, a kitty litter trap and walls, Turn 4 at Laguna Seca is *not* where you want to first be experiencing the sensation and having to deal with it!)

Accelerate through corner.

Note abrupt rise in pavement at corner exit. Wide open throttle here.

Put two right wheels across top of stripes, track out to left edge, then transition right to mid track.

The Club Corner

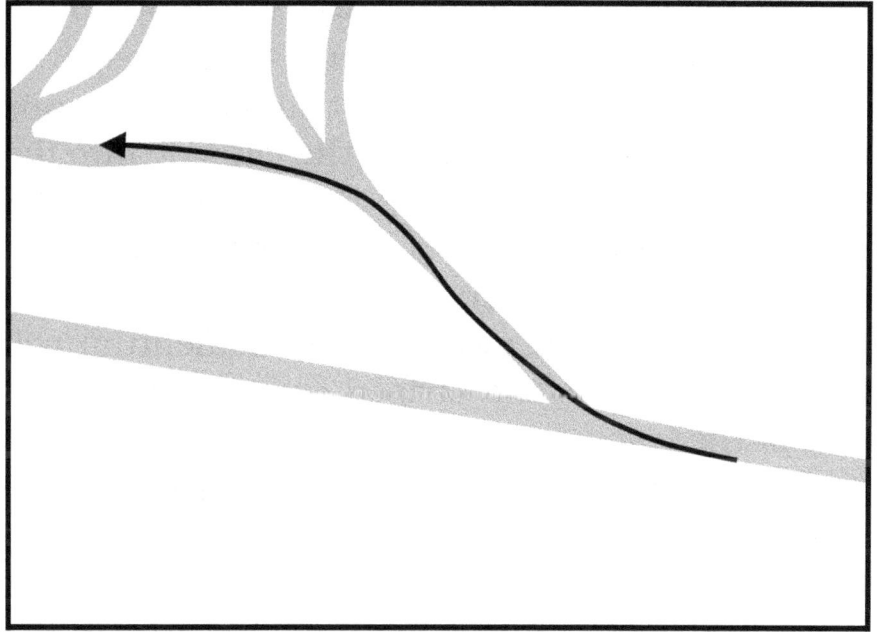

The approach to Club Corner is WOT in almost all cars. A crisp angle turn on the map, you will of course "round out" the corner with the widest radius arc that you can. Wait for the turn in to be sure you late apex the corner, use the flat red and white stripe painted inside berm or curb ahead on the right as your target, put both of the right side wheels right across the top of it and stay down on the throttle. This may take some practice as you are going to be in fourth or fifth gear accelerating as though you were on a straight segment coming out of Grapevine. You will track all the way out to the left edge on exit from Club Corner, continue your curved driving line to move back across the track to the right edge, then follow the sweeping right to left sweeper corner towards the Bus Stop.

Smooth transfer of inertial loading/weight is key here, smooth in gently transitioning your loading on the suspension to the left side into the Club Corner, then from the left side to the right side so you can stay on throttle all the way through the sweeper. As you cut through the corner apex on the right to left sweeper the momentum will take you towards the striped berm on the right side of the track surface.

(**Beginner's note:** You may find that a little breathe off the throttle is called for as you figure out the driving line on entry to this segment through the Club Corner, and again through the right to left sweeper. That is fine. Remember, just because "everybody" says the preferred method is to go through this segment at WOT doesn't mean in fact you actually should! "Everybody" is not you, nor are they driving your car. The real question is "preferred method for whom?"

Be safe and develop your own judgment about what you can handle competently. Going through a corner five miles per hour slower than your actual maximum potential and working up towards the limit in small increments is much better than going into it one quarter mile per hour faster than you can handle, thus going on a high speed off track excursion. Remember that the maximum potential is not a constant. From hour to hour the conditions of the surface, your tires, your car, and yourself as the driver... will change, thus affecting what you can and cannot do. Developing this skill of self awareness will be one of the most important attributes you can acquire for both speed and safety. If you are missing your driving line in Club Corner, you are probably missing the driving line elsewhere, and you need to consider whether it is time for a driver rest break.)

Late corner apex and sweeping exit to right edge to set up entry for Bus Stop turn.

Note how curb bends right towards cones (don't follow it) while corner entry is left.

Stay far left and use all available track surface.

The Bus Stop Turn

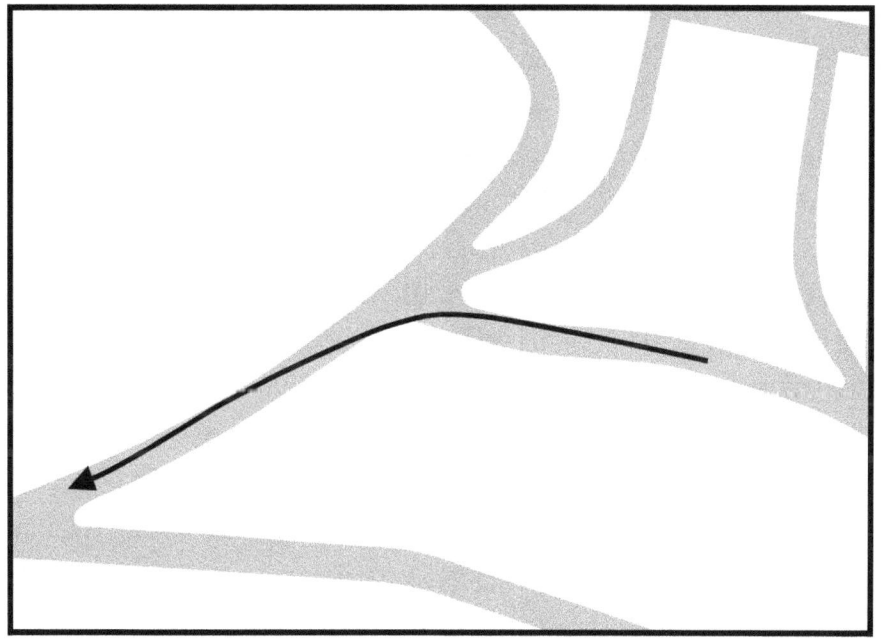

At this point you will have tracked out to the right and have a subtle little bend from left to right at the end of the Club Corner segment, followed by the hard lefty known as Bus Stop. A challenging corner with great reward, and risk, for negotiating it quickly, your set up for *corner entry* to Bus Stop is critical. You are carrying a lot of speed as you approach Bus Stop, and you want to smoothly straight brake on the right edge to slow the car down to the maximum entry velocity that you can carry while turning through the corner, and put some loading on the front right tire as you make your turn in. But don't smash down on the pedal and compress the front so there is nothing left in the suspension to give for the corner.

Grip is key, the corner is quick as a wink, and trail braking or rotation is not advised. Getting on throttle too soon or too hard can pitch the car's weight backwards... and remove critical grip from your steering on track out to the right. You don't necessarily want to fully follow the track's pre-corner bend to the right following the striped berm before turn in, as it will force you to increase the number of degrees you must change direction from right to left and shorten the radius of the arc of your turn, and thus slow you down.

Instead, you want to open up the radius by describing an arc from the right edge of the track surface next to the berm but pointing a few degrees to the left rather than parallel, then cutting hard left across the top of the inside berm and having your momentum carry you all the way to the right edge. Do not put the right side tires on the painted berm because it is more slippery than the asphalt and may have less grip as you brake and then turn.

Putting the left side tires over the top of the painted berm at the corner apex is less of a concern as the weight is almost all transferred to the right side tires, and the berm is almost flat and does not tend to upset the balance of the car. It is keeping the car on the pavement and not tracking out too wide to the right on corner exit that is the challenge here.

At the limits of adhesion, an under steering car will "push" the front off the edge, and an over steering car will waggle its tail "loose" off the edge, and this turn is an excellent diagnostic of handling balance for the machine. It is also a fine test of driver skill in controlling the weight balance front to rear and managing the car whatever its behavioral inclinations. A lot of drivers wind up raising dust clouds through the Bus Stop.

(**Beginner's note:** 'This is a technically complex turn that puts a premium on driving line, braking timing, precise corner turn in timing, weight transfer (side to side and front to rear), and throttle control, all compressed in a *very* short section of pavement and time. Unlike the Grapevine turn, this is not a place to feel frisky, even though there is plenty of run off room. Speed is high and recovery potential with counter steer if you "overcook" entry or time your turn in too late is almost nonexistent. Ride with your instructor and pay careful attention to this segment. Work on getting through this corner smoothly and consistently, understand what work the car is doing, and only very gradually increase speed through it.)

Track out has right side wheels loaded heavily. Do not drop them in the loose dirt off the edge.

Transition from Bus Stop to about mid track, then set entry to corner apex on right under hard throttle.

Truckstop and the Riverside Sweeper

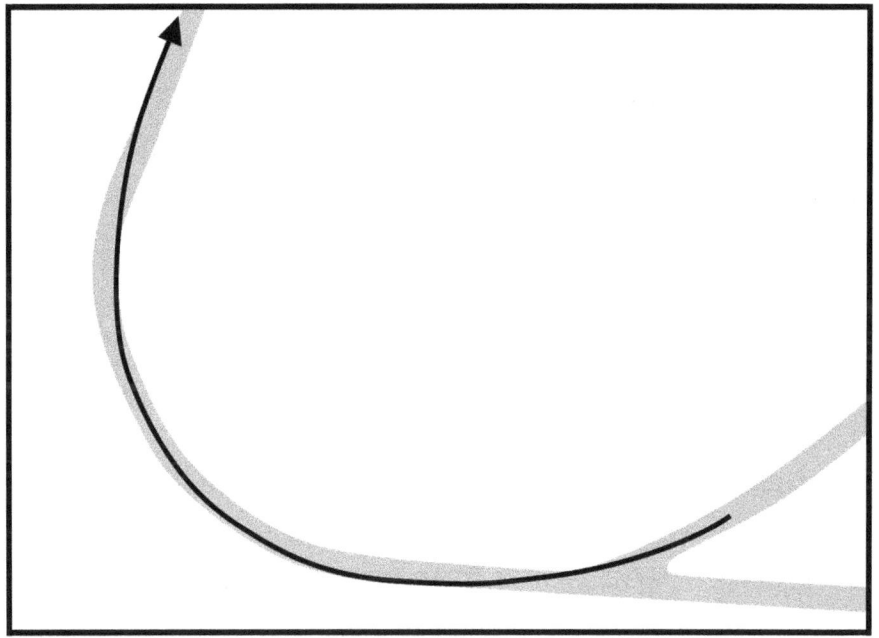

Having successfully hung on to the right edge of the track surface for Bus Stop, we keep squeezing throttle on as we unwind steering lock and move left, but not all the way to the left edge, before we set up for the Truck Stop corner, which really is just the entry chute to the fast Riverside sweeper. From about mid track you cut crisply right on the apex at Truck Stop, still accelerating constantly, and track out to the edge of Riverside at the "top" of the turn, to get a very wide radius arc and ultimately a super late corner apex coming out of Riverside Sweeper, with a corner apex point at perhaps 3/4 to even 7/8 of the way through the sweeper depending on your car and track surface conditions.

This is another "tire adhesion test" corner, but at very high speed, well over 100 mph for many high horsepower cars. The corner is a slightly downhill accelerating sweeper that will have you maintaining throttle at grip limits, and gradually rolling on even more to WOT as you cross the apex point and begin to unwind the steering. There is a bit of positive camber working for you into the apex point, but that positive camber rolls away immediately thereafter and you track out to the left briskly under throttle. That kind of speed with any type of lateral inertial force is potentially dangerous, so leave a margin for safety on the left edge, and do NOT apex early or you will run out of track on the left very fast, and at a most unpleasant rate of speed.

(Beginner's note: This is not the place to experience throttle on over steer or to flirt with running off the left edge at track out. Fortunately, if you are driving on street tires, and the track surface is dry, the long steady turn will tend to set the tires to a steady howling well before they start to lose grip, and even DOT-R rubber will "talk to you" before letting go of their grip. Listen to the tires, feel the car through the turn, concentrate on keeping your eyes up, looking out towards the exit apex to the corner, and through that apex to the track out point on the left edge, resisting the temptation to turn in early.

Hold on the steering lock at the corner apex so you gracefully and continuously begin to transition placement of the car from the left edge at track out to the center right of the track following track out. If you are driving a car that does not have a modified suspension, it is likely that the car will have the factory programmed handling under steer, so a traditionally reflexive lift of throttle will pitch weight forward, helping to regain steering grip while also slowing the car.)

Track out left from Truckstop, then settle into wide arc sweep at mid to two thirds from inside edge.

Full throttle through late apex. Lateral inertia will push car to left edge so hold steering a bit longer.

TRUCKSTOP AND THE RIVERSIDE SWEEPER 61

From left edge continue to hold steering and transition to center of track for entry to next corner.

You are going fast here. Mark apex on left.

Snug on apex, but high speed will push car to right edge, then transition back to left edge.

Set up for late entry on left edge. Note cone marking apex at top right of hill.

Approach to Phil Hill

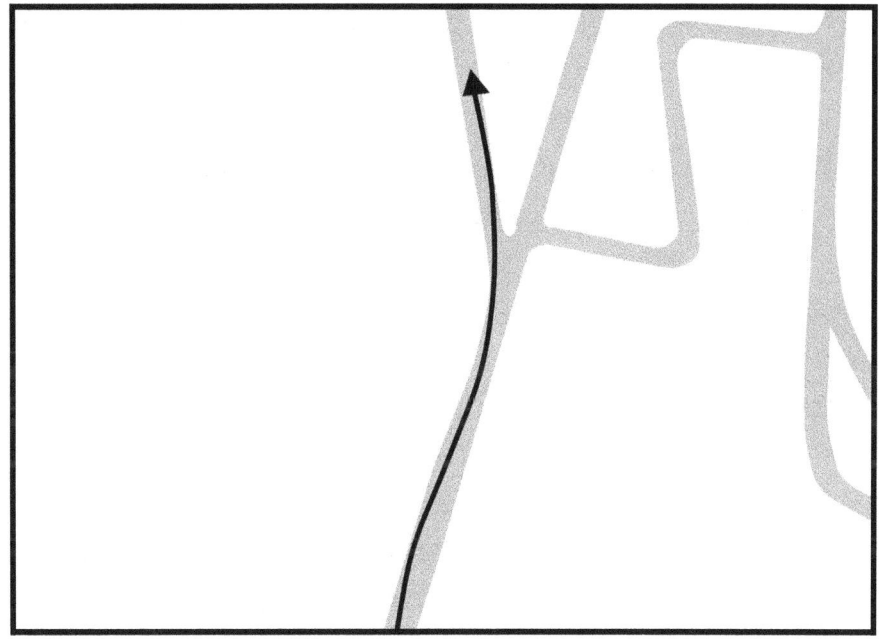

Now going at or close to WOT after exiting Riverside and having tracked out to the left edge, we stay down on throttle and ease back to the right in a continuous transition off the left edge. There is no time to dally, and you want the car to follow a gentle "S" from left to right and then back again, cutting over the striped berm on the inside left edge apex of the unnamed angled corner leading to Phil Hill, another man made pile of silt covered in a ribbon of asphalt that delivers an approximately 20 foot elevation change.

The speed here is now well up, having gone WOT from just before apex at Riverside all the way down the following short straight segment (even though we do not go straight down it!) and curving through the angled corner towards Phil Hill. Get the car suspension to take a "set" on the right to left turn in for this corner when moving at high speed, so use very smooth and flowing input to the wheel, nothing quick or jerky. After cutting left across the apex point, the car will track well towards the right edge from the high speed. Keep the smooth rhythm of steering and weight transfers, hold right to left steering input, and smoothly transition your driving line all the way back to the left edge, while still keeping the throttle to the floor, then straighten out along the left track edge, straight brake and down shift before commencing your turn in to Phil Hill.

(**Beginner's note:** Upon completing your track out from Riverside it is very easy to pause, looking down the long straight ahead, steadily accelerating, only to realize the right to left turn is coming up and the radius of the arc through the turn is too tight and you are at risk of running out of track on the right edge after the corner unless you lift throttle or brake. Accordingly, remember to immediately be transitioning to get your car repositioned to at least mid track after exit from Riverside and before turn in so that the right to left turn is smooth and wide even though you are going quickly. Concentrate on moving the weight from the left side to the right side deliberately and without being too jerky or sudden such that it upsets the balance of the car.)

Apex on right edge at top of hill. Straighten steering a touch and on throttle.

Left edge, beginning sweep to right edge.

Full throttle, late turn in to corner apex.

Phil Hill

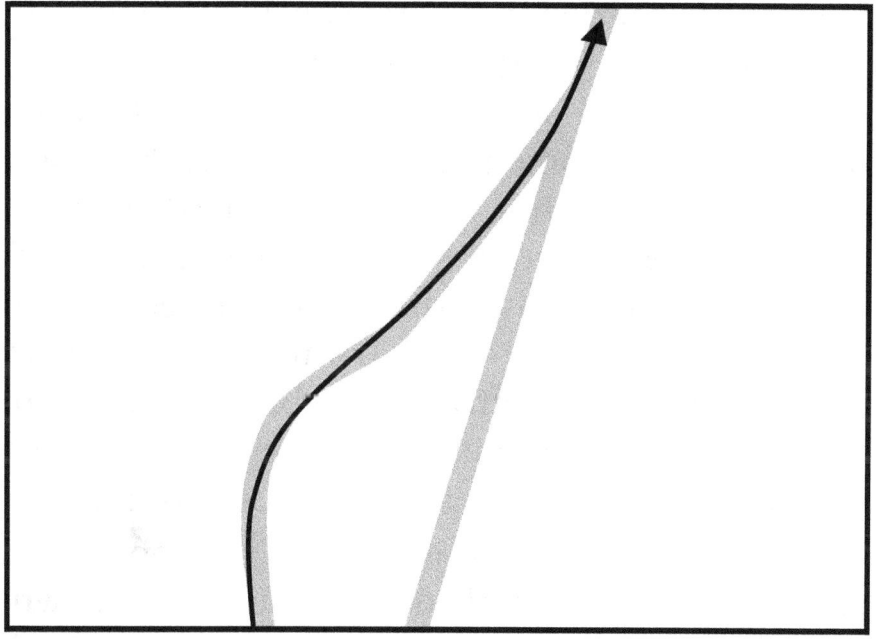

There are two bits to this corner, the left to right corner itself and a little right to left kink at its exit. The Phil Hill corner (named in honor of America's first Formula 1 champion and consultant on the design of the Buttonwillow circuit) is apexed at the crest of a sharp incline that is on positive camber going up, and off camber coming down, with the crest line at a sharp angle to the direction of the car as a result of the left to right corner configuration. So, once again, we do not want to be braking after commencing turn in, the turn in should be late, and we want to straighten out the front steering wheels going over the angled crest so that when we come over the top and are light in the rear and off camber, the back of the car does not throw itself out to the left.

Be ready for a quick counter steer input to the left as you come over and down the crest. Work on having the momentum carry you to the inside of the next turn but without the need to input much recovery counter steer, or steering from left to right to keep you on the track surface, so you can put all of the grip from the tires into acceleration as soon as possible, rather than having to save some grip for steering out of the turn by going at less than maximum speed.

Done right you will drop over the top of Phil Hill, be hard on throttle as the rear settles down, and clip across the inside apex of the little kink right to left corner at the bottom of the hill under WOT. Do it wrong and you may lose the rear to the left and possibly leave the track sideways into the dirt, raising a monstrous cloud of dust and at risk of a roll over.

(Beginner's note: You must have the correct angle of approach. Do not be in a hurry to go fast through this segment, because you can wind up going off track on the left, and sideways as you approach the bottom of the hill, which is a "bad thing", especially since the ground is soft and might grab a wheel and flip the car over. Concentrate on getting the driving line right and very gradually working up speed here, as well as getting the feel for what the car does when it gets "light".)

Late apex keeps car on left edge to set up for entry to Sweeper.

Begin turn in to either mid or right edge entry line.

Middle driving line at corner entry.

Approach to the Sweeper

From the center right of the track as you approach the turn, up shift and carry on your track out from the Phil Hill towards the right edge, then as you reach the turn in point (which is likely to be about two car widths or more away from the right edge) make your right to left turn in, still without lifting throttle as the surface merges with the wide section of the track that is shared with the drag strip.

(**Beginner's note:** The surface here is very wide and you will not need to use all of it even in a very fast car. Ease back to the left edge, check your mirrors and gauges quickly, let faster cars by on the right, and prepare to brake before entry to the Sweeper.)

Ease to two thirds from right edge. Head swiveled right to fix corner exit apex.

Note how late exit apex presents, and pinch of left side edge. Angle of approach is to left edge by lead car.

Sweeper

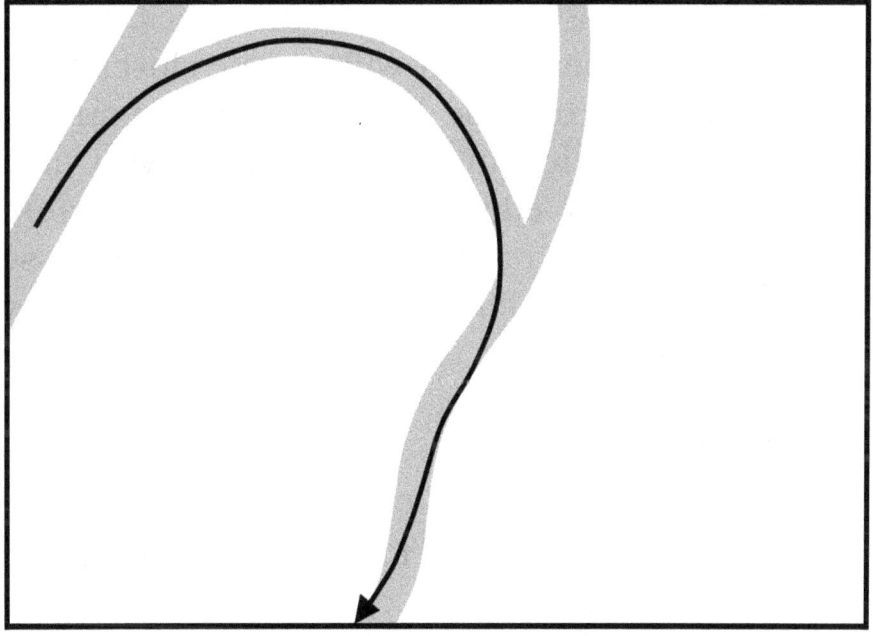

You will be WOT as you approach the Sweeper, holding the throttle down until you reach your braking point, and then begin a steady straight brake and down shift as you prepare for turn in to the Sweeper. This is a higher speed at entry corner that starts off like a classic 180 degree and wide radius sweeper corner... but beware... it does not finish that way. And because it does not finish that way, there is more than one way to take the corner.

The more classic approach to Sweeper is to place the car about mid track entry for a steady turn, using the "tire talk" to help you manage your speed limits. Do not hug the inside right edge. As you approach the end of the corner it tightens down abruptly into a diminishing radius and finishes more like a corner of 200 degrees. As you set up for the apex the car will now be closer to 2/3 or 3/4 out from the inside edge. If you are carrying two much mid corner speed you may creep to the left edge and drop wheels before reaching the corner apex, or more frequently lose the track on the left edge at corner exit by approaching the apex too early and being at the wrong angle. (In this regard it is not unlike Turn 9 at Willow Springs, just at less than half the velocity of that notorious corner.)

Some racers with well tuned suspensions and the ability to control some extended slip will employ a "double apex" attack to the corner, and carry more speed into a right edge corner entry, going deep in to the mid corner and drifting to about 2/3 out from the inside edge of the track, then apply some trail braking and rotate the nose of the car to the inside right, and hold against the drift with a touch of counter steer. This puts the nose angle deeper into the apex and allows earlier and harder acceleration on exit without running off the track surface on the left. Needless to say, that is a skillful maneuver by experienced drivers, and unless you have that car control ability as second nature, it is not an option for you.

A very late proper apex, using either approach successfully, sets you on the left edge of the track surface at corner exit and up on the striped berm, with the nose of the car aimed squarely at the entry to the Esses. You are immediately WOT as soon as you are straightened out and all of the grip of the tires can be applied to acceleration. Anything early on apex either puts you in the dirt, or backing off throttle, or even braking or waggling as you try to catch up to the geometry of the corners, destroying your next long run. So be patient and get your technique right first, before you charge hard through Sweeper.

(**Beginner's note:** This is definitely a corner that rewards the patient and prepared driver who swivels their head and sets his/her eyes well ahead of the direction the nose of the car is pointed in the corner, and who then steers to the apex point. You will instinctively follow your eyes to the corner apex point and significantly reduce the chance of being surprised at a sharp turn coming at you with not enough track to work with. Some advance study of the geometry of the corner and focus will help you stay on the surface here.)

Hold to surface and track along left edge.

The Esses

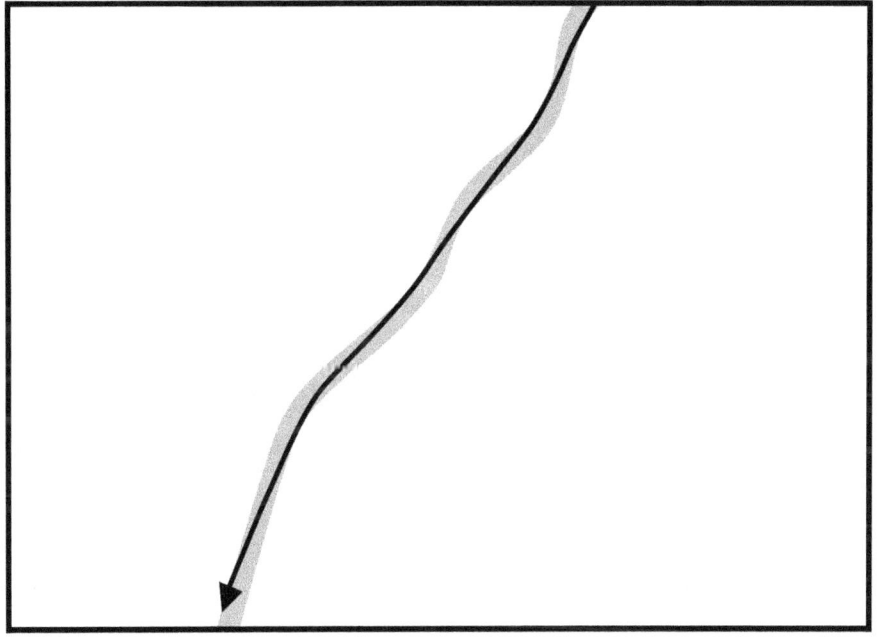

Moving through the Esses you will be WOT all the way through, attempting to gently and yet steadily move the weight of the car from side to side, kissing and not running high over the top of the rather tall striped berms, straightening out as much as possible the run between the second-third-fourth corners, timing your up shifting in the brief straight section between the berms, and concentrating on setting up the exit apex on the fifth and last right to left corner, which is the most important because it leads you to a long straight.

It is a good idea to check your mirrors in the straight section between the first and third Esses to locate the relative position and rates of closure of cars behind you since your approach to the Sweeper. As you finish your "straight" run between the first and third of the Esses, smoothly work some steering input into the third so that you will be pointing just a bit more to the right from the "straight" line that you were taking. This will open up the radius arc for the last one. That apex on the last of the Esses must be late. Otherwise at WOT in a medium to high horsepower car you can run out of track on the right edge in fourth or fifth gear, which is a very dangerous situation with the concrete wall off track on your left. That wall may look far away, but in fact cars have planted themselves nose first into that wall, as the grassy ground cover between the track and the wall is slippery and provides little braking assistance. If you are running DOT-R compounds or slicks as your tires, you will have as much ability to control your direction on grass as an archer does after the arrow has left the bow.

The error of running off is compounded when the driver tries to correct and as soon as the right wheels regain traction on the pavement, the right to left steering input yanks the car hard left and launches the driver perpendicularly across the track to explore the effectiveness of the car's crumple zone and safety harness set up on the left wall.

(**Beginner's note:** If you drop two wheels, or four, on the right side exit of this corner, do not fight your way back on to the track surface with abrupt steering, nor jam on your brakes, with two wheels on pavement gripping hard and two wheels in the dirt slipping and sliding. Instead, lift smoothly out of the throttle, hold the steering straight, and depending on your situation gently drive straight into the run off area and slow down or stop, and wait for a clearing of the inevitable cloud of dust so that you can safely see traffic, while also looking at the flag station at the track exit to the pits for signals of all clear.

The alternative, if it is safe because you have been watching your mirrors and know that nobody is behind you, and you are not badly out of shape on exit, is to coast back on to the track with a gradual easing back on to the surface, applying hard throttle only after all four wheels are back on the asphalt. Be ready for a potential quick lurch left as the right side tires regain grip with a quick counter steer to the right, and a gentle squeeze of throttle to settle the back end down and help prevent it from coming loose and turning you into a spin. Ease back where the edge is as close to the level of the dirt as possible, so you don't cut the inner sidewall against the asphalt edge and blow out your tires. It is likely that if you go off, it is where many others before you have done the same, and there is a depression in the dirt that may be two inches or more. So you don't want to attempt to immediately steer back on if there is that much difference between the two surfaces. If you do spin, then immediately go "two feet in", clutch and brake, and ride it to a complete stop, hopefully in a safe spot. When you lose control, the best thing you can do is get it stopped as soon as you can, covering as little distance as possible. When you go two or more wheels off, it is advisable to get into the pits for a safety inspection to remove any pebbles that may have lodged between the rim and the tires, or between the brake rotor and brake pads.)

Set up from left edge to make turn in and enter first of the Esses at angle to "straighten" run into segments 2 and 3.

Note entry angle has opened up the "eye of the needle" and car can negotiate nearly straight line with minimum lateral transfers.

Prepare for gentle turn to right to set up for 4th segment.

Apex of fourth segment is late. Increase radius of corner by exiting third segment towards center of track.

Wider angle of attack from late apex opens track out and allows higher corner exit speed without running out of surface on the right.

Exit to right and proceed along right edge.

Riverside. It is the responsibility of the overtaking car to complete a safe pass.

Prepare for the Unexpected

A few words about safely getting by a suddenly distressed car in front of you. This section of track at Buttonwillow presents a good spot to remind ourselves that all of us are out on a track to have a good time as safely as possible. But sometimes events will unfold that are not on the menu of "good time", and you need to be prepared to deal with them.

Most of the occasions on track when a car gets into difficulty that presents a potential or actual risk to others, the corner workers at their flag stations and connected by their radio sets to each other will be signaling track conditions in front of you that allow you to take appropriate and safe measures to manage the hazard. Know the flags!

Most events involving an off track excursion or other hazard transpire from start to finish in a matter of only a few seconds, and somewhere other than right in front of you. With typical track lengths of 2.5 to 3.5 miles and lap times of between 1:45 and 3:00 minutes, you often have an abundance of time and space to be warned and prepared. By the time you arrive at the scene, the car involved may already be back on track and on its way such that you never even see it before it reaches the track exit. Or the last wisps of dust and tire smoke are wafting away and the car is stationary.

But eventually, and it could be your first day out or your fiftieth, somebody is going to "lose it" in front of you in close enough proximity that advance corner worker flag signals are not relevant.

You are on your own judgment and skill to avoid disaster, and it is on you immediately.

It could be a loss of control by the driver of that car. It could be the surprise of a part falling off such as a lug nut, exhaust pipe, body panel, even a drive shaft, or a fluid being discharged from a blown coolant hose or engine oil. It could be a small animal bolting across the track, or a plastic bag blowing on to your windshield. It could be you losing your brakes, or having other control problems. Your engine may quit, clutch pedal stick to the floor, or steering fail. All things mechanical can break, and many of them do break.

One may recall an all wheel drive turbocharged car losing a piece of its exhaust from the undercarriage at an HPDE at Buttonwillow immediately in front of a following car through this section. This was followed shortly by the melting of enough parts to start a little fire in the underbody of the lead car. Nobody was hurt, the car was not severely damaged, the fire was put out by the fire crew, and the alert corner workers immediately put out the debris warning flag, followed by the "black flag all" for the other drivers. But it certainly was no fun and there was no warning for the following car. At near triple digit speed a violent evasive maneuver was out of the question, and there was no time or space anyway; just hold steady and go over it. Fortunately the piece was small enough that it went straight under the car without striking anything vital, but even if it had, it is better to have some car damage than rolling out of control off the track surface. There was time to then get the arm out the window to give the track exit signal, merge to the left and take the track exit, then proceed to the pits and jack up the car for a thorough safety inspection to confirm that in fact no contact with the debris was made and nothing was bent, broken, cut or sliced.

Desert tortoises are known to have crossed the track at Spring Mountain in Pahrump ("How did that boulder get in the road... it wasn't here a lap ago?"), fresh water crayfish in Turn 4 at Laguna Seca, and armadillos, deer, dogs, possum, raccoon, coyote, squirrel, jack rabbit and other creatures are not uncommon jaywalkers on many circuits elsewhere. Wet leaves, pine needles, dust and grit, rubber marbles, not to mention oil, water, coolant, brake fluid, steering fluid... the possibilities of surprise challenge are without limit. You don't get to choose, you must be ready for anything. Every lap is new and different and you must be focused in your concentration without lapses.

If you are following another car, even at a distance of 20 or 30 car lengths, you should have them in your vision clearly as your head should be up. The Esses at Buttonwillow reflect a classic corner where as you are coming to the apex of the fourth of the Esses and preparing for your turn in to the fifth and last, you should be monitoring the car in front and aware of whether it has negotiated the track out on the right edge successfully. If that car in front has dropped one or more wheels off the right edge, you have time to back off the throttle and give room and time for the events in front of you to unfold, including if necessary to slow down or stop or even deliberately leave the track surface should that be the safest alternative left available to you.

You should not assume that because the car in front of you has drifted off to the right that it is safe to pass on the left or that the other driver is even aware of your presence. Indeed it should be presumed that the driver ahead has his/her hands very full with the challenge of car control and has lost all focus on everything else. With the risk that they could compound their track out error of running off the right edge with an overcorrection that launches them across the track from right to left, hammering the throttle and taking a path to the left could simply cause one of you to go nose first into the side of the other in a violent collision. As the overtaking car it is your responsibility to manage a pass safely. You have the advantage of being in control of your car and seeing everything in front of you, while the car in front of you does not. Accordingly, with your priority being safety, and not the achievement of your personal best lap time on this lap, slow down.

This does not mean that you should slam on your brakes and create a second potential hazard to cars approaching from behind, and a compounding of the danger and complexity of safe passage. Rather, with the knowledge of who is behind you and how close from having checked your mirrors on approach to the Sweeper and again in the "straight" between the second and fourth of the Esses, you begin your safe evasion of the problem in front.

If the driver in front exhibits a controlled exit and slowing off track to the right, safely pull off line to the left and pass, then merge back on the driving line to the right edge and set up for the Sunset Corner. If the driver in front is spinning on the track surface, apply brake smoothly and slow down while carefully watching the direction of his momentum and what the car is doing. If he/she is "both feet in" and sliding to the left edge, stay right and manage your speed to be able to take safe evasive action if there is a sudden and unexpected change in the direction or dynamic of the car in front, such as a roll or flip or sudden regaining of traction so that you can stop without colliding.

You want to get safely by the event if you can, so that approaching cars from behind are not an additional danger to you or the car in trouble. Once you are past the event and out of immediate danger yourself, you can follow the directions of the corner workers, which may be a simple yellow flag caution, or a black flag to all drivers to come in to the pits under caution, or even a red flag to all drivers to come to a full and complete on course stop until directed to restart.

What a lot of your study to driving a course efficiently does is highlight the places where not only you might get into trouble, but where other drivers are likely to get into trouble and how and why. You should analyze what you ought to do as a driver should that trouble occur to you, so that you have prepared for it and can react quickly... there is no time for leisurely reflection in the midst of the challenge. You should know where the run off areas are, where the walls or other obstacles are. You should have already determined what you need to be doing and why and how before you ever get there. You should also have maintained sufficient track awareness that you know whether there are cars approaching from behind so that your recovery efforts are going to be among the safer options.

That preparation for what you are going to do if you get in trouble also helps you to understand what the likely dynamics of a car in front of you are going to be should it be in distress, and what is likely to transpire as the driver struggles for control, so you can act accordingly as the following car to avoid further mishap to either of you. This should be a part of your preparation and study for driving every corner on every course before you strap in to your car to drive it. And then closely note in your orientation laps with your instructors, and in your own warm up laps, the action options and whether they match up to your expectations from your track map reviews, in car videos you have watched and discussions with other drivers

If the sponsor organization offers an orientation ride around the track for drivers, by all means do it. Even better, do try to get the opportunity to walk or bicycle around the track. A slow, close up look at the track will reveal subtle undulations, changes in camber, surface grip conditions, run off area characteristics and much more. If you can do it with four or five other drivers, you will pick up much valuable information during your conversation as you journey around the circuit.

Note late entry by lead car into positive camber corner.

Camber flattens on track out. Early apex here can put you off surface on right.

The Sunset Turn

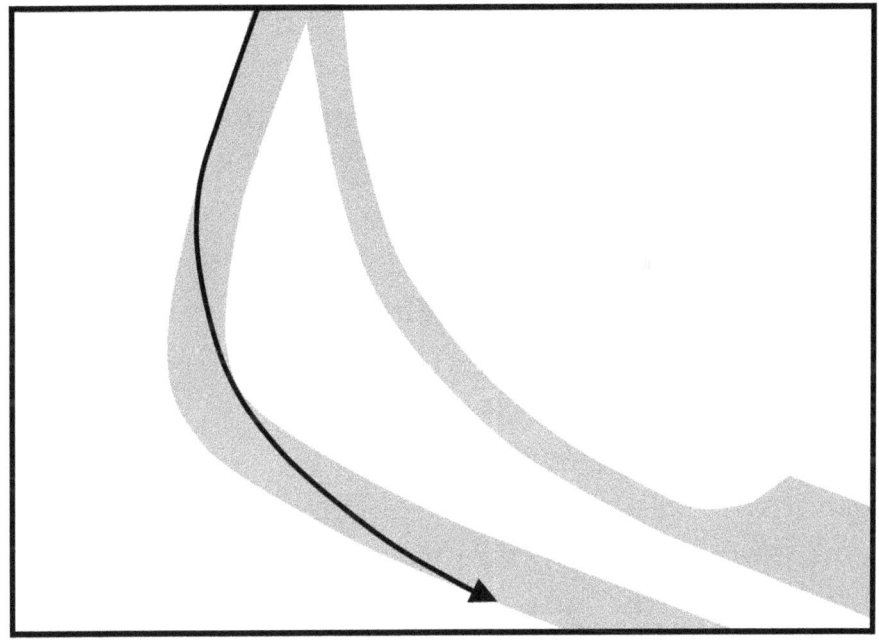

Proceeding down the right edge of the track at WOT in fifth gear, you approach the last corner of the lap, the "Sunset" Turn. This is perhaps the most "overcooked" corner on the circuit, following a long high speed segment, and leading to the front straight. The temptation to carry maximum speed through this almost 90 degree corner is great, leading to entry speeds that are too high, and apexes that are too early. This combination results in many cars exiting the right edge at high speed on corner track out and with a very high cloud of dust.

There is positive camber down low in the corner, but it rolls away quickly, promoting a lot of drift inertia off right, similar to the last of the Esses described above, and with the pit wall looming cross track on the left, with similar potential adverse consequences. What distinguishes this corner from the Esses however is that the problem is typically initiated with a failure to brake early enough, to bring the speed down to the right entry velocity.

(**Beginner's note:** Picking your braking inception point is very important, as is waiting for a late turn in. "Slow in-fast out" is a very important mantra to repeat to yourself for this corner, and you have time to remember and recite it as you hurtle towards Sunset after exiting the Esses.)

Straight brake, downshift, and advanced drivers can trail the brake just a touch and rotate the rear a few degrees with some counter steer, then take the low-late apex route and accelerate hard through the corner and track out to the right edge for your fastest possible run to the start/finish line.

Track Exit

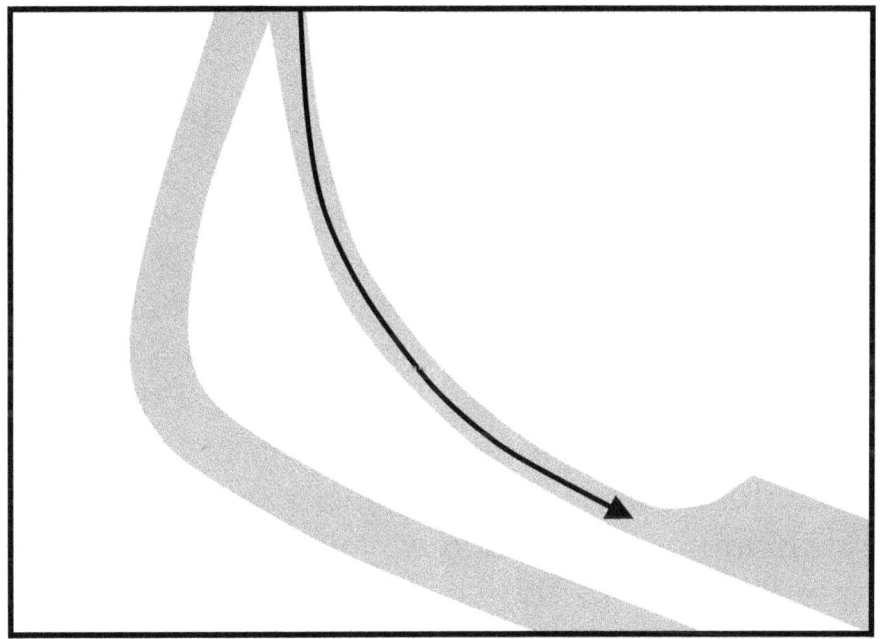

Exit from the track is on the left edge, between the Esses and the Sunset Turn. Because the driving line takes the car down the right edge of the track surface to set up for entry to the Sunset Turn, the set up for exit from the track is very clear and clean.

Upon exiting the Esses and tracking out to the right side at full speed, and having safe control of your car, get the left arm out of the window to give the track exit signal and promptly, but smoothly, move your car to the left edge of the track surface. As you slow to a safe track exit lane speed the cars coming from behind will be all the way across the track on the right side of the surface, with plenty of room for them to make passes between them going down the straight.

The danger of the exit procedure is if there is a car hard on your rear coming into or out of the Esses, as the passing line will be for the overtaking car to move left to the inside of you as you both enter the straight, potentially blocking your ability to move across the track to the exit lane. There is plenty of distance before the exit lane. There are a couple of ways to approach this issue. If the overtaking car is gaining in the Esses, but will not catch you before track out, you may reduce your speed slightly in the last of the esses such that you will not track out all the way to the right, and can smoothly move to the left edge, giving the track exit signal. This way the pursuing car will see the signal, follow the racing line on track out and proceed unimpeded up the straight to the Sunset Turn.

If the overtaking car is closer and aggressively makes or may make its move to pass on you, do not give the track exit signal, which will cause confusion for both of you on just who is supposed to be doing what, where, and when. Instead, stay on the driving line, give a point by signal to the left side, and just make a light lift off throttle after they make the passing move on the left side to help them make the pass more quickly, then give the track exit signal, safely move behind the passing car and transition left across the track to the exit lane on the left edge.

If there are multiple cars in a "nose to tail" line behind you, prefer the first option as you might not be able to let them all by while hugging the right side, and your slowing enough to then get back across to the exit lane before running out of room could present a danger, both to you as a slow moving hazard, and to the late passing car that will have limited room to get back on to the driving line on the right edge after passing you to make the proper braking run before turn in.

(Beginner's note: High variance in velocities is dangerous to all cars involved. They promote a fast rate of closure and limited time to react. The driver immediately behind you has a great view of you and what you are doing or signaling, but the car next in line has very limited or no view of you at all. Don't be creating the potential for surprises with erratic driving behavior. The drivers behind will all be expecting a car on the driving line to be driving quickly, not putt-putting along. You should have awareness from the straight section leading to the Sweeper of whether cars are behind you, how many, and how far and what rate of closure there is. Then, coming out of the Sweeper and getting through the Esses you can quick check the rear mirror again before approaching the last of the Esses to make your decision on how to manage your track exit procedure.)

Track out to right edge and down the straight.

Distinguishing Characteristics

By now it is rather apparent that the Buttonwillow circuit tests and rewards the patient driver who properly prioritizes the importance of the respective corners, and recognizes the value of carrying maximum exit speed from key corners all the way through the ensuing segment until he/she is obliged to once again touch the brake.

Buttonwillow demands the driver apply thinking skills to get around the circuit quickly. This applies not only to corners classically followed by straights, but also corners followed by segments that carry through other corners that can be negotiated at WOT or close to WOT. (Grapevine to Bus Stop, Bus Stop to Phil Hill, Phil Hill to Sweeper, Sweeper to Sunset.)

Selective application of trail braking can also be of benefit, in slow corners such as Offramp and Cotton Corners, in medium speed corners with camber advantage like Sunset, and complex corners like Sweeper).

Heel and toe downshifting technique is very much rewarded, left foot braking may be applied in Grapevine, Bus Stop, Riverside and Sweeper, and where a skilled driver has command of the car through loading and unloading the suspension both front to back and side to side can provide very fast negotiation of certain segments at what for the novice would appear to be insanely fast speeds.

Hard braking, but without upsetting the car's balance, with transition to sharp corners is required into Sunrise, Offramp, Cotton Corners, Phil Hill, Sweeper and Sunrise.

The thrill of high speed is found in the front straight, the approach from Club Corner to Bus Stop, the Riverside Sweeper, the approach to Phil Hill, the approach to the Sweeper and the approach out of the Esses down the straight to Sunset Corner.

The track is very flat overall and provides good driver visibility through and beyond most corners, at the cost of having only two elevation challenges that are man made and modest, but still interesting.

Conclusion

This is a track that will keep a driver very busy at the controls, with approximately 23 corners in three miles, and plenty to be learning and polishing skills over, for all levels of driver skill and car capability from low power "momentum" racers to big power brutes.

Buttonwillow's versatility in both configuration and directional driving options makes it an outstanding circuit for both teaching and competition, for a wide array of types and classes of cars and skill levels of drivers. It is fast enough to have the thrill of speed, rewards skillful techniques with the controls, as well as the ability to balance the car smoothly from side to side and front to back, while overall presenting a reasonably safe level of road course challenge.

Reflect for just a moment, that all of the driving decisions described above, and more, will transpire in a single lap, compressed into about two minutes, as contrasted to the considerably longer time that it took you to read a summary description. And will be repeated ten to twelve times in a single session of HPDE driving, without pause or respite physically, mentally or emotionally. And you will have four, five or even six sessions available to you in a single day of driving.

Whether you are a novice working to learn your skills, or seasoned expert driver working to polish them to a fine hone, Buttonwillow is an excellent driving circuit well able to please drivers at all skill levels.

Approach to Offramp. Note angle of entry to corner. Lead car tracking out from apex.

Closing Note on Driving Lines

There is much more to determining the optimal driving line (and braking inception points, corner turn in points, corner apex points, track out points, etc.) than just an exercise in geometry on a flat road map. Because that is only the starting place for developing the "best" driving line for you.

Track conditions will influence your evaluation of the line to take. What is the weather? Is it cold or warm? Is it dry, humid or even wet? What is the condition of the surface in any given location of the track? Is the camber positive, negative or neutral? Is the surface ascending or descending?

The car you are driving will influence your evaluation of the line to take. What type of car are you driving, how heavy is it, what is the weight balance of the car, where are the drive wheels, what type of suspension (springs/ dampers/ control arms/ camber adjustments/ anti sway bars/ strut towers/ bushings), what type of tire and tire compound, inflation pressure, tire size, how much horsepower/torque, what type of slip differential, what type and size of brakes/ brake fluid/ pads do you have?

Who is driving will influence the evaluation of the line to take. What is your experience, what are your skill sets, how familiar are you with the particular track, what is your physical condition, are you mentally sharp and focused today? Now add to this the fact that many of these factors are variables that change throughout the course of the day, indeed some of them through the course of a single session. Accordingly the purpose of the driving lines presented in this guide are to give a general orientation for you to become familiar with the track and then promptly develop your own before you begin to push your personal envelope that day. Obviously, novices should not be "pushing" anything other than the priority of having a fun safe day by staying well under the limits of performance for the track, the car, and themselves. This guide is not written to teach driving. There are many other excellent books that address technique, and excellent driving and racing schools. I encourage you to explore both to the fullest of your ability to do so, as they will enhance both your safety and enjoyment of high performance driving.

Track Checklist

Minimum Required of All Run Groups

- ❏ Helmet. Snell rated SA 2000 or better. Motorcycle helmets are not acceptable.
- ❏ Tech Inspection form
- ❏ Car Numbers – required on both sides of the car and rear, a minimum of eight inches high – this can be with blue painter's masking tape – any self adhering but removable and re usable numbers, vinyl or magnetic, must not peel off at high speed
- ❏ Tow hook installed (preferred) or tow point clearly established
- ❏ Long sleeve cotton shirt and full waist to ankle cotton pants (Cotton or Nomex clothing ONLY. No leather or synthetics allowed. This includes underwear).
- ❏ Closed toe shoes, preferably with a thinner sole for improved pedal feel, cotton socks
- ❏ Torque wrench, lug nut socket that fits your wheels
- ❏ Tire pressure gauge

Highly Recommended for Intermediate and Advanced Groups

- ❏ Driving Suit of not less than two layers, preferably three layers, fire resistant Nomex

- ❏ Race Driving gloves
- ❏ Race Driving shoes
- ❏ Nomex socks, undergarments, balaclava
- ❏ Face shield for helmet
- ❏ Fire Extinguisher, fixed within reach of seated and belted driver
- ❏ Neck brace, collar or Hans Device
- ❏ Racing seat or bucket
- ❏ Properly installed harness system of five points or more, three inch or more belt width.

Optional Supplies

For the Driver:

- ❏ Drinking water or electrolyte drinks. No alcohol drinks permitted on track site at any time. No smoking anywhere in the garage or pit areas.
- ❏ Hat – for Sun
- ❏ Sunglasses
- ❏ Sun Screen
- ❏ Folding chair
- ❏ EZ-UP Canopy
- ❏ Hand Soap/clean wipes
- ❏ Ice chest
- ❏ First aid kit
- ❏ Map/directions/phone number of hotel
- ❏ Map/directions/phone number of track
- ❏ Camera
- ❏ Camcorder/mount

For the Car:
- ❏ Extra Brake pads
- ❏ Brake fluid – one bottle
- ❏ Engine Oil – two quarts
- ❏ Power steering fluid – one bottle
- ❏ Coolant-Radiator- one gallon
- ❏ Distilled Water – Radiator- one gallon
- ❏ Duct tape – one roll
- ❏ Painter's tape – one roll
- ❏ Glass cleaner – You will kill some bugs on your way to the track. You may collect rubber streaks from "marbles" and more bugs on the track
- ❏ Brake Bleeder line and collector bottle
- ❏ Hose Clamps- assorted sizes
- ❏ Zip ties – one dozen
- ❏ Work gloves, heat resistant
- ❏ Jack – as light a weight yet strong as you can find
- ❏ Two foot long wood 2" X 4" stud
- ❏ Jack stands (2) minimum
- ❏ Jumper Cables or Jump starter box
- ❏ Service manual
- ❏ Other tools (sockets, wrenches, pliers, screwdrivers, allen keys...)
- ❏ Utility knife, multipurpose tool, scissors
- ❏ Grease
- ❏ Paper Towels – one roll
- ❏ Clean rags - six
- ❏ Trash bags - two

- ❏ Run Flat aerosol cans
- ❏ Tie Wraps
- ❏ Stopwatch
- ❏ Race tires and wheels, one set
- ❏ Spare tire
- ❏ Tire pyrometer
- ❏ Flashlight
- ❏ Funnel for oil
- ❏ Gloves – disposable
- ❏ Air compressor for tires
- ❏ Data logger
- ❏ Transponder
- ❏ Two way radio/walkie-talkie set
- ❏ Bucket
- ❏ Chamois
- ❏ Bug cleaner/degreaser
- ❏ Mild car soap
- ❏ Car sponge

Tech Inspection Form

Driver:_____ Date:_____

Make:_____Model:_____

Year:_____ Color:_____Stock or Modified:_____

Note: If you are self-teching your car, it is your obligation to physically check every item on this form. Do not assume your lugs are tight, re-torque them to make sure. This checklist is for your safety and the safety of the others on the track with you, and should not be dismissed as a formality. If the item is "good" mark with a check. If it is not, write "NO" and call it to the attention of the registrar, and support will be found to assist you to address the issue. After teching your car, you must sign the bottom of the form (in both places if you're self teching), which indicates that you have, in good faith, checked every item on this form. Please bring this form with you to the track, or you'll have to do a new tech at the track before you will be allowed on the track, possibly missing your first run group.

WHEEL and TIRES
Street Tires:
❏ More than 2/32" of tread?
Race Tires:
❏ Good condition/no cording?
❏ Cuts or other defects?
❏ All lugs present and torqued?
❏ Hub/Center-caps removed?

ENGINE
❏ Any fluid leaks?
❏ Wires/hoses secured ?
❏ Throttle return springs tight?
❏ Radiator overflow OK?
❏ Battery properly secured?
❏ Battery terminals covered
   (rubber boots / duct tape OK)?
❏ Fluid lines OK?

BRAKES
❏ Pedal pressure firm?
❏ Fluid level correct?
❏ Lines OK?
❏ Brakes lights working?
❏ Pads more than 5mm?
❏ Rotors OK (no cracks, etc.)?

STEERING & SUSPENSION
❏ Wheel bearings OK (no play)?
❏ Steering tight?

BODY
❏ Gas cap OK?
❏ Body panels secure?

SAFETY EQUIPMENT
❏ Helmet approved?
   (Snell 2000 or newer, M or SA)
❏ Seats secure?
❏ Long sleeve cotton shirt?
❏ Closed-toed shoes?
❏ Seatbelts properly installed?

APPROVED SEATBELTS
The following systems are approved:
(Please check one)
❏ OEM 3-Point
❏ 5 or 6-Point
4-Point*
*All 4-Point systems must pass fech at the event.
*4-Point Belts inspected by:_____

Note: Mark each line with a check (✓) if that item is OK; write "NO" if that item is not OK.

Print Name: _____ Signature: _____

Dedication

This book is dedicated to the many people that this adventure in high performance driving has brought me together with, past-present-future, and that I would never have otherwise met. The fraternity of drivers at HPDE has been steadfastly friendly and supportive in these early years, with helpful advice in learning courses and driving, shouldering jacks and pushing cars on and off trailers, even sharing parts and tools when necessary. All with a genuine shared enthusiasm for the sport, and a concern for the safety and well being of each other on and off the track. I hope with this effort to give back to our growing community a resource that will encourage safety, responsibility and development of skills so that all involved, both experienced and novice, will stay safe and well as they pursue their passion for driving.

Acknowledgement

Many thanks to Steve Staveley, former Regional Executive of the California Sports Car Club, and to Oli Thordarson, competition driver and sportsman, for their generous time in reviewing this work and providing their excellent expert insights, perspectives and suggestions for additional elements to include or emphasize in this text. One cannot have more knowledgeable support than from those who have years of experience on their home track and base of operations. And thanks for their enthusiasm and encouragement not only for this title, but to continue with the series of titles addressing the excitement of experiencing high performance driving education on America's road racing circuits. We all have busy "day jobs" (how else can we get the funds to buy more "go fast" parts?), and their responsiveness and depth of thought and reflection on top of their already crowded schedules is characteristic of the comraderie within the fraternity of drivers, as well as the desire so many of us have to participate in communicating to the community of enthusiasts detailed information to help everyone prepare better for safe, enjoyable days of motorsports.

Photo courtesy of Sammy Davis Photography–Los Angeles, CA

About the Author

Edwin Reeser is just another one of the millions of motorsports enthusiasts, who devotes entirely too much time, energy and funds to the passion of high performance driving. You too will have reached this point when 1) you won't supersize your french fries order for a few additional pennies but think nothing of spending another $1,500 for a high flow exhaust, 2) accept the logic of the racer's adage "if you are under control you are not going fast enough", and 3) have no emotional reaction to substantial cosmetic or mechanical damage to your car, when you formerly would have had hysterical upset from a door ding, other than concern over how long will it take before you can get back on the track.

Other Race Track Attack Guides from Sericin Publishing released in 2010:

Laguna Seca - Monterey, California

Willow Springs International Motorsports Park - "Big Willow" - Rosamond, California

Auto Club Speedway - Auto Competition Course with "Roval" - Fontana, California

Reno Fernley Raceway Park - Configuration A - Fernley, Nevada

Thunderhill Raceway Park, Willows, California

Track guides in preparation for future release:

Sears Point Raceway, Sonoma, California

Las Vegas Motor Speedway, Las Vegas, Nevada

Spring Mountain Motor Sports Ranch, Pahrump, Nevada

Willow Springs International Motorsports Park - Streets of Willow, Rosamond, California

For more information go to:
www.RaceTrackGuides.com

www.ingramcontent.com/pod-product-compliance
Lightning Source LLC
Chambersburg PA
CBHW072200100426
42738CB00011BA/2480